Nita Mehta's

Different ways with

PASTA

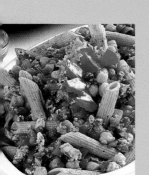

Nita Mehta's

Different ways with
PASTA

Nita Mehta

B.Sc. (Home Science), M.Sc. (Food and Nutrition), Gold Medalist

SNAB
Excellence in Books

Nita Mehta's

Different ways with
PASTA

SNAB
Excellence in Books
Snab Publishers Pvt Ltd

Corporate Office
3A/3, Asaf Ali Road, New Delhi 110 002
Phone: +91 11 2325 2948, 2325 0091
Telefax: +91 11 2325 0091
E-mail: nitamehta@nitamehta.com
Website: www.nitamehta.com

Editorial and Marketing office
E-159, Greater Kailash II, New Delhi 110 048

Food Styling and Photography by Snab
Typesetting by National Information Technology Academy
3A/3, Asaf Ali Road, New Delhi 110 002

Recipe Development & Testing:
Nita Mehta Foods - R & D Centre
3A/3, Asaf Ali Road, New Delhi - 110002
E-143, Amar Colony, Lajpat Nagar-IV, New Delhi - 110024

© Copyright SNAB PUBLISHERS PVT LTD 2008-2011
All rights reserved
ISBN 978-81-7869-190-9
Reprint 2011

Printed in India by Aegean Offset Printers, Greater Noida

Distributed by :
NITA MEHTA BOOKS
NITA MEHTA
BOOKS
Distributors & Publishers
3A/3, Asaf Ali Road, New Delhi - 02

Distribution Centre :
D16/1, Okhla Industrial Area, Phase-I,
New Delhi - 110020
Tel.: 26813199, 26813200
E-mail: nitamehta.mehta@gmail.com

Contributing Writers:
Anurag Mehta
Tanya Mehta
Subhash Mehta

Editors :
Sangeeta
Sunita

Price: Rs. 295/-

Cuisine has traveled faster than any other aspect of our life-style. Certain foods are now a common phenomenon in the kitchens worldwide. Probably the most popular one is Pasta.

Pasta is a 'hot' and 'cold' favourite of all households. This book gives pasta lovers loads to experiment with. It gives away the secret of flavours and aromas that one always thought were beyond one's skills. Pasta is easy to cook and quick to serve. It can be used as an appetizer, a whole meal, as a salad or a snack. Pasta recipes are easy to follow and the dishes look aesthetically great when served. It has also become a very popular dish amongst children and they can be easily lured into eating just by serving pasta!

INTRODUCTION

Contents

PASTA 8

PASTA IN RED SAUCE 16

VEGETARIAN

NON-VEGETARIAN

PASTA IN CREAMY SAUCES 46

UNUSUAL PASTA RECIPES 77

PASTA SALADS 89

GLOSSARY 96

Pasta

Pasta comes in countless shapes and sizes. It is very difficult to give a definite list, as the names for the shapes vary from country to country. The most common names have been listed.

TYPES OF PASTA

1. Lasagne Sheets
2. Bow Pasta/Farfalle/Butterfly Pasta
3. Gnocchi
4. Spiral Pasta/Serpentine Pasta
5. Penne
6. Fussili
7. Rigatoni
8. Tagliatelle/Ribbon Pasta
9. Cannelloni
10. Capelli/Angel Hair Pasta
11. Spaghetti
12. Shell Pasta
13. Fettuccine

How to Boil Pasta

Ready-made and homemade pasta are cooked in the same way, though the timings vary greatly. Homemade pasta takes more time cook. Freshly made pasta can be done as little as 15 seconds after the cooking water comes back to the boil. Stuffed pasta takes a few minutes longer. When done, turn the pasta into the colander (chhanni) and proceed as for dried pasta.

To Boil Ready-made Dried Pasta...

Pasta can be bought in dry form and can also be made fresh at home. The dried one is easily available in packets and has a long shelf-life. Fresh pasta is not easily available, so the recipes have been provided. It is suggested to use the dried one, because it is very handy and quite good in taste. The fresh one comes out perfect if you have the pasta making machines.

1. To cook 2 cups of pasta, boil 8-10 cups of water (½ of a big pan).
2. In the water, add 2 tsp salt and 1 tbsp olive oil or any cooking oil. Drop pasta in boiling water.
3. Stir in between so that pasta does not stick to the bottom of the pan. Boil, stirring occasionally, for about 7-8 minutes till pasta turns almost soft, but yet firm. Do not overcook. Remove from fire and leave pasta in hot water for 3 minutes.
4. Strain. Refresh it with cold water. Strain. Leave for 15 minutes in the strainer for the water to drain.
5. Pour evenly 1 tbsp olive oil on cooked pasta to prevent it from sticking. Toss gently. Use as required.

Making Fresh Sheets of Lasagne and Cannelloni

This is a fresh pasta recipe for lasagne sheets & cannelloni. The dried form is easily available in the market. The authentic recipe is with eggs but this one has been adapted to suit the vegetarians too (without using egg).

1 cup maida (plain flour)
4 tbsp oil, ¼ tsp salt

1. Mix all the above ingredients in a shallow bowl (*paraat*) and knead into a firm, but smooth dough, using a little water. Knead well for 5 minutes.

2. Cover the dough and keep aside for 30 minutes in the fridge.

3. Divide into 4 balls with greased hands. Roll out a ball, on the kitchen platform to a size of about 10" x 6", or as thinly as possible to a very thin sheet. Use cornflour instead of maida, for dusting while rolling. Cut sheets to neaten the edges. Cut for lasagne or cannelloni according to the size of the baking dish.

4. Boil plenty of water in a large pan with 2 tsp salt and 1 tbsp oil and cook 2-3 sheets at a time, for about 2-3 minutes, till the pasta rises to the surface and is done. Do not let the sheets turn too much while boiling.

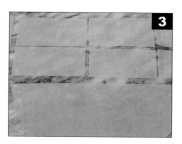

TiP

We set the pasta dough aside for 30 minutes to let the gluten in the flour relax. If not done, you run the risk of making hard pasta.

Tips for Cooking Pasta

These are a few simple guidelines to ensure pasta is cooked to perfection.

PASTA IS COOKED TILL IT IS 'AL DENTE' ?

Pasta is cooked to the "al dente" stage - This means it is tender but with firm resistance to the bite. To test, press a piece against the side of the pan with a fork. It should need a firm pressure to break the pasta. Over cooking makes it mushy and it breaks, losing it's shape. Cooking time varies according to the size and shape of the pasta and also whether it is thick or thin.

HOW MUCH DOES DRY PASTA INCREASE IN VOLUME ON COOKING?

1½ cups dry pasta becomes 2¼ cups on being cooked. So, dry pasta increases in volume on cooking. Whereas, fresh pasta does not absorb much water, so it does not increase much in volume on cooking.

HOW MUCH PASTA SHOULD BE BOILED AT A TIME ?

It is best not to cook more than 675 gms pasta at a time, even if you have a very large pan, because of the danger in handling a large amount of boiling water.

DO DIFFERENT SHAPES OF PASTA HAVE DIFFERENT COOKING TIME?

Cooking time varies according to the size and shape of the pasta and also whether it is fresh or dried. Fresh pasta cooks very quickly, often the boiling time being only 3-5 minutes, and is ready when it rises to the surface of the boiling water. Dried pasta takes longer; allow about 7-8 minutes but stir frequently.

SHOULD ONE IMMEDIATELY REFRESH COOKED PASTA WITH COLD WATER?

After it is removed from fire, the cooked pasta is strained and refreshed under tap water. This is done to stop the cooking process in the pasta. This help the pasta to remain crunchy without getting mushy.

HOW TO PREVENT PASTA FROM DRYING OUT ?

If pasta is not be used immediately, sprinkle some oil on it and mix gently.

IF THE PASTA DISH APPEARS TOO DRY AT THE TIME OF SERVING, WHAT SHOULD BE DONE?

Add some fresh cream or milk to it.

HOW TO ENHANCE THE FLAVOUR OF PASTA DISHES?

Before adding the sauce, if the pasta is tossed in a little butter or olive oil with oregano, red chilli flakes and some crushed peppercorns, the taste is enhanced. You can add some freshly chopped parsley to add colour and flavour.

WHENEVER I BAKE PASTA IT TURNS DRY?

When pasta is to be baked, cover it completely with sauce and then cheese, so that the pasta is not exposed to direct heat, which makes it turn stiff and hard. Secondly, cover it with aluminium foil and then bake especially in the case of cannelloni, lasagne or ravioli.

WHAT SHOULD BE THE CONSISTENCY OF THE SAUCE?

The sauce should be thick enough to coat the pasta. Extra runny sauce is not desirable with pasta. The sauce should coat the pasta without disappearing through it.

CAN ALL SHAPES OF PASTAS BE BAKED ?

Although pasta can be simply tossed in butter or olive oil and some hot sauce poured over it and served, it can also be baked along with vegetables. Usually baked dishes are made of lasagne and cannelloni. However, all the small pastas like penne or macaroni can also be baked.

WHEN SHOULD THE PASTA BE ADDED TO SAUCE?

Pasta tends to absorb a lot of liquid or sauce it is put in. So pasta should be put in sauce only at the time of serving. You can prepare the sauce & keep it aside, otherwise pasta absorbs the sauce and tastes dry.

A LIBERAL DASH OF OLIVE OIL OR ANY OTHER COOKING OIL ADDED WHILE BOILING IS HIGHLY RECOMMENDED! WHY?

It prevents the pasta from drying out.

HOT! HOT! HOT!

Serve any pasta dish the moment it is ready. Pasta tastes best when served really hot.

HOW TO PREVENT BOILED PASTA FROM DRYING OUT ?

If pasta is not be used immediately, sprinkle some oil on it and mix gently.

A SPECIAL TIP!

Reserve pasta water when straining boiled pasta. Use the strained water if using water anywhere in the recipe instead of plain water.

TiP

LEFTOVER PASTA TURNS DRY THE NEXT DAY.
To regain the freshness of the pasta dish, add about ¼ cup milk to a serving of 4 and cook for 2 minutes. Serve hot.

About Ravioli and Gnocchi
(Fresh Pasta)

RAVIOLI [rav-ee-OH-lee; ra-VYOH-lee]

An Italian speciality of little square- shaped or round pillows of dough with fluted edges, filled with any of various mixtures such as cheese or vegetables. Ravioli are boiled, then sometimes baked with a cream, cheese or tomato sauce. These are usually square but size and shape vary enormously. The filling can be anything from vegetables such as spinach, artichoke and mushroom to mixed veggies etc. The recipe to make ravioli follows later in the book (page 27).

GNOCCHI [NYOH-kee]

Small, soft Italian dumplings (ripple-edged shells). They can be made with semolina or potato dough or flour. Eggs or cheese can be added to the dough, and finely chopped spinach is also a popular addition.

They are shaped like oval shells. The best-known type of gnocchi are *gnocchi di patate* from northern Italy, made with potatoes and a little flour. Gnocchi are generally shaped into little shells, cooked in boiling water and served with butter and Parmesan or a savoury sauce. The dough can also be chilled, sliced and either baked or fried. The recipe to make gnocchi follows later in the book (page 70).

How to Make Garlic Bread

a French loaf or any long loaf of bread

GARLIC SPREAD
6 tbsp softened butter
½ cup grated mozzarella cheese
2 tbsp olive oil
2-4 flakes of garlic - crushed
¼ tsp pepper
½ tsp red chilli flakes
½ tsp oregano

1. Cut the bread into diagonal slices of ½" thickness.

2. Put all the ingredients of the garlic spread in a big bowl. Beat well with an electric hand mixer.

3. Spread the mix on all the slices.

4. Bake in a preheated oven at 200°C for 10 minutes or till the bread turns crisp on the edges and bottom. Serve immediately.

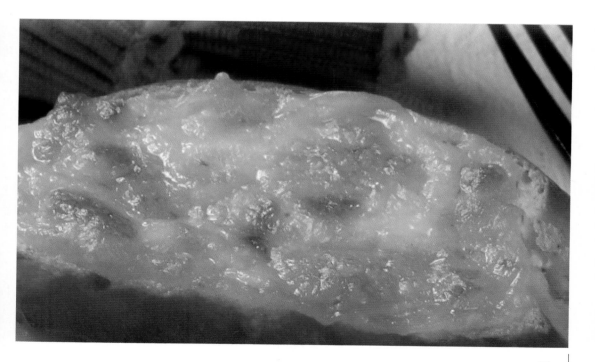

PASTA IN RED SAUCE

Sicilian Carrot Capsicum Pasta

I once made this as a side dish for dinner and it was good.

Serves 6

2½ cups dried elbow macaroni shells, 8 medium sized tomatoes
2 capsicums, 5 tbsp olive oil or butter, 2 large onions - chopped (2 cups)
1 carrot - thinly sliced or coarsely chopped (½ cup)
2 tsp crushed garlic, 1 tsp fennel (*saunf*) - crushed, 1 tsp crushed pepper, 1 tsp salt
½ cup grated cheddar or mozzarella cheese (optional)

1. Boil 8-10 cups of water in a large pan. Add 2 tsp salt and 1 tbsp oil. Drop pasta in boiling water. Boil for 7-8 minutes or till pasta turns soft but is still firm. Remove from fire and let the pasta stay in hot water for 2-3 minutes. Strain. Refresh in cold water and strain again. Leave pasta in strainer for 15 minutes so that all the water drains out. Sprinkle 1-2 tbsp olive oil on the pasta and toss well. Keep aside.

2. Put whole tomatoes and capsicum in boiling water for 3-4 minutes. Remove from water. Peel the tomatoes. Puree tomatoes and capsicum in a mixer.

3. Heat oil in a pan. Add onion, carrot and garlic, cook for 5 minutes.

4. Add pureed tomatoes, fennel, pepper and salt. Bring to boil, reduce heat for 6-8 minutes. Add pasta and cheese. Mix well. Serve hot with garlic bread.

Chicken Cacciatore Pasta

Easy to make, this simple pasta is delicious to eat.

Serves 4

250 gms chicken (boneless) - thinly sliced

2 cups serpentine or any other dried pasta

3-4 tbsp oil, preferably olive oil, 2 tsp finely chopped garlic

1 large onion - finely chopped (1 cup)

½ cup ready made tomato puree

5 large tomatoes - blanched (put whole in hot water for 10 minutes till soft), skinned and churned in a mixer to get puree

¼ cup white wine or strained pasta water

1 tsp vinegar (or to taste), preferably balsamic vinegar

1 bay leaf (*tej patta*), 2 tsp dried oregano

1 tsp dried thyme (optional), 1 tsp sugar, ¾ tsp pepper

1 tsp salt (or to taste), 4-6 black olives - halved (optional)

1 tbsp chopped fresh parsley or coriander

1. Boil 8-10 cups of water in a large pan. Add 2 tsp salt and 1 tbsp oil. Drop pasta in boiling water. Boil for 7-8 minutes or till pasta turns soft but is still firm. Remove from fire and let the pasta stay in hot water for 2-3 minutes. Strain, reserving the water. Refresh pasta in cold water and strain again. Leave pasta in strainer for 15 minutes so that all the water drains out. Sprinkle 1-2 tbsp olive oil on the pasta and toss well. Keep aside.

2. Heat 2 tbsp oil. Add chicken pieces and cook on moderate heat till it is nicely browned for about 5-6 minutes. Remove the chicken and keep aside.

3. To the same oil, add 1 tbsp more oil & chopped garlic. Fry till it starts to change colour.

4. Add chopped onion and cook till soft, not brown.

5. Add chicken, fresh and ready made tomato puree, wine or strained pasta water, vinegar, bay leaf, oregano, thyme, sugar, pepper and salt. Add another ½ cup strained pasta water. Boil. Lower heat and simmer for 10 minutes till the sauce becomes thick. Keep aside.

6. At serving time heat the sauce, add boiled pasta, olives & chopped parsley. Mix well. Sprinkle some freshly crushed peppercorns. Serve hot with toasted buns or bread.

Pasta Mexican Wave

Add any of your favourite vegetables to this quick lunch recipe –
and add chilli, if you can take the heat!

Serves 3-4

2 cups penne pasta - boiled, 1 green capsicum - sliced into fingers
¾ cup ready-made corn kernels, ½ cup grated mozzarella or pizza cheese

SAUCE
3 tomatoes, 2 onions - chopped finely, ½ cup ready-made tomato puree
1 capsicum - chopped finely, 2-3 green chillies - chopped finely
4 tbsp chopped coriander leaves, 2 tbsp lemon juice
1 tsp oregano, 1 tsp salt, 1 tsp cumin (*jeera*) - powder
1 tsp paprika powder or degi mirch

1. Boil 8-10 cups of water in a large pan. Add 2 tsp salt and 1 tbsp oil. Drop pasta in boiling water. Boil for 7-8 minutes or till pasta turns soft but is still firm. Remove from fire and let the pasta stay in hot water for 2-3 minutes. Strain, reserving the psta water. Refresh in cold water and strain again. Leave pasta in strainer for 15 minutes so that all the water drains out. Sprinkle 1-2 tbsp olive oil on the pasta and toss well. Keep aside.

2. Boil whole tomatoes in water for 3-4 minutes, or till soft. Drain. Cool. Peel and chop the blanched tomatoes.

3. For sauce, heat 3-4 tbsp oil. Add chopped onions and cook till soft.

4. Add all the remaining ingredients of the sauce. Mix well and cook for 3-4 minutes.

5. Add 1 cup reserved pasta water. Boil. Cover and simmer for 10 minutes. Remove from fire. Let it cool. Churn in the mixer to get a smooth sauce. Keep aside.

6. To serve heat sauce in a pan, add pasta, capsicum, corn and sprinkle cheese. Mix gently. Serve hot.

Red Thai Chicken Pasta

This is a Thai pasta, which evidently gives full spicy flavours of the Thai curries. Thai lovers try it.

Serves 4

3 cups gnocchi pasta or any other pasta - boiled
200 gms boneless chicken- sliced into ½" flat pieces
3 tbsp oil, 1" pieces cut french beans (½ cup)
2 cups ready-made coconut milk
1 tsp brown sugar or ½ tsp regular sugar, salt to taste

RED CURRY PASTE

8 Kashmiri red chillies - seeded & soaked in ¾ cup warm water for 10 minutes
1 onion - chopped, 15 flakes garlic - peeled
2" piece ginger - sliced
2 stalks of lemon grass or rind of 2 lemon
3 tbsp coriander seeds (*dhania sabut*)
2 tbsp vinegar, 2 tsp cumin (*jeera*)
12 peppercorns (*sabut kali mirch*), 2 tsp salt

1. Boil 8-10 cups of water in a large pan. Add 2 tsp salt and 1 tbsp oil. Drop pasta in boiling water. Boil for 7-8 minutes or till pasta turns soft but is still firm. Remove from fire and let the pasta stay in hot water for 2-3 minutes. Strain. Refresh in cold water and strain again. Leave pasta in strainer for 15 minutes so that all the water drains out. Sprinkle 1-2 tbsp olive oil on the pasta and toss well. Keep aside.

2. Roast coriander and cumin till light brown.

3. Grind all the ingredients of the red curry paste along with the roasted ingredients using the water in which the chillies were soaked, to a very fine paste.

4. Heat 3 tbsp oil in a pan, add red curry paste and fry for 3 minutes on low heat.

5. Add chicken and 2 tbsp of coconut milk, stir fry for 5-6 minutes on medium heat.

6. Add the rest of the coconut milk.

7. Add beans, salt and sugar. Cook for 3-4 minutes. Add pasta and mix well. Serve hot.

Note: For vegetarian pasta omit chicken and add 200 gms of mushrooms, or increase the quantity of beans.

Eggplant Tomato Lasagne

Two favourites – lasagne and eggplant are combined in one delicious dish. What could be better? Just lasagne sheets with lots of sauce. Cover the whole dish with foil while baking. And you require no preparations like boiling the sheets.

Serves 2

5 dried lasagne sheets, each 3" broad and 6" long
1 cup grated mozzarella or pizza cheese

FILLING - 1
3 small eggplants (*baingan*) - cut into ¼" round slices
salt, 2 tbsp olive oil

FILLING - 2
150 gm cottage cheese (*paneer*) - roughly crumbled
5 tbsp finely chopped parsley or coriander
½ tsp salt, ½ tsp black pepper
½ tsp cumin (*jeera*) powder

SAUCE
1½ tbsp oil
½ tsp crushed garlic
½ tsp pepper, ¼ tsp oregano
1 cup ready-made tomato puree, ½ tsp salt

1. Place the eggplant slices in a colander, sprinkle with salt and cover with a plate and keep aside to sweat for ½ hour. Rinse well and pat dry on a clean kitchen towel.

2. Preheat oven to 180°C/350°F.

3. Heat 2 tbsp oil in a big pan, add 6-7 eggplant slices at a time and cook until lightly brown on both sides, about 5 minutes, cooking in batches. Remove eggplant onto a large plate lined with paper towels. Keep aside.

4. Mix paneer, parsley, salt, pepper and cumin powder in a bowl!.

5. For sauce, mix all the ingredients together in a bowl. Cook for 3-4 minutes in a pan or microwave for 2-3 minutes.

6. Spread 2 tbsp of the tomato sauce at the bottom of the baking dish.

7. Wet a pasta sheet under running water. Place sheet on the sauce in the baking dish.

Contd...

8. Spread 2 tbsp sauce on the sheet. Cover all edges. Sprinkle ¼ of the paneer on the sheet. Arrange ¼ of the fried eggplants. Sprinkle some mozzarella cheese.

9. Place a wet sheet on it. Again layer with sauce then paneer and lastly eggplants. Sprinkle mozzarella before placing the next sheet. Continue layering till you reach the last sheet. Top generously with sauce and then cheese.

10. Cover with foil. Place the lasagne in the pre-heated oven at 180°C and bake for 25-30 minutes or until the top is slightly golden and when you stick a knife into it, the knife comes out clean. Uncover and bake for 10 minutes to get a golden top.

11. It's best to let the lasagne set for at least another hour before serving, as this "plumps" the pasta. Reheat before serving.

12. To serve, cover with foil. Cut into squares and serve.

Tips...

Leaving the Lasagne to stand before serving makes it easier to cut.

Always cover the lasagne with foil before baking. This prevents the sides of the sheets from drying out.

Ravioli in Barbeque Sauce

Read about ravioli a little before beginning the recipe on page 14.

Serve 4

1 cup plain flour (125 gms)

¼ level tsp salt

2 eggs

1½ tbsp butter

½ egg (whisk one full egg and divide it into, ½ and use as required)

BARBECUE SAUCE

2 cups water

2 tbsp Worcestershire sauce

3 tbsp tomato ketchup

½ tsp red chilli powder

½ tsp paprika or degi mirch

2 tbsp vinegar

2 tbsp brown or regular sugar or to taste

1 soup cube - crushed

3 tbsp cornflour mixed 6 tbsp water

FILLING

½ cup corn kernels

¾ cup grated cottage cheese (*paneer*)

¼ tsp red chilli flakes

¼ tsp salt

¼ tsp oregano, ¼ tsp pepper

2 tbsp chopped capsicum or coriander

1. Sift the flour and the salt into a mixing bowl & make a well in the centre. Lightly beat 2 eggs and pour into the flour; mix thoroughly. Melt butter in a small saucepan and add to the flour. Knead the mixture to a stiff dough with a little cold water.

2. Turn the dough on to a floured surface and knead for 10 minutes until shiny. Set it aside to rest for at least 1 hour.

3. Mix all ingredients of the filling in a bowl.

Contd...

4. Roll out the dough, on a floured surface, to a paper–thin 24" square. With a tea spoon , drop the filling over one half of the square, at intervals of 1½". Brush between the fillings with lightly beaten egg. Turn over the other half of the dough and press down firmly with the fingers between the fillings. Cut through the space between the filled squares with a pastry wheel. Dust the ravioli squares with a little flour and set them aside for at least 1 hour before cooking.

5. When ready for cooking, bring a large pan of lightly salted water to the boil. Drop the ravioli into the water and cook for about 7 minutes. Drain and sprinkle 1 tbsp oil, toss well and keep aside covered till serving time.

6. For sauce mix all the ingredients of the barbecue sauce together in a bowl. Give one boil. Add cornflour paste and cook till slightly thick for about 2 minutes. Do not cook further. Remove from fire. Keep aside till serving time.

7. To serve toss ravioli lightly in the sauce. Serve hot.

Indian Makhani Pasta

A quick – and exceedingly tasty – vegetarian version of the classic makhani gravy. This dish is easy to prepare and makes a very satisfying meal.

Serves 4

2½ cups dry shell pasta - boiled

1 packet baby corns (125 gms) - slit each piece into two pieces, or 1½ cups corn kernels

SAUCE

3 tbsp oil, 1 tsp crushed garlic, 1 tsp ginger paste

1 cup ready made tomato puree

2 tsp dry fenugreek leaves (*kasoori methi*)

½ tsp garam masala, 1 tsp deghi mirch powder

½ tsp red chilli flakes, 1 tsp salt (to taste)

¼ cup cream, ¾ cup milk

CASHEW AND SPICE PASTE (GRIND TOGETHER)

¼ cup cashew (*kaju*) - soak in hot water for 10 minutes

½ tsp pepper (*kali mirch*) powder

a tiny blade of star anise (*chakri phool*)

1 tsp black cumin (*shah jeera*)

¼ tsp cinnamon (*dalchini*) powder

1. Boil 8-10 cups of water in a large pan. Add 2 tsp salt and 1 tbsp oil. Drop pasta in boiling water. Boil for 7-8 minutes or till pasta turns soft but is still firm. Remove from fire and let the pasta stay in hot water for 2-3 minutes. Strain. Refresh in cold water and strain again. Leave pasta in strainer for 15 minutes so that all the water drains out. Sprinkle 1-2 tbsp olive oil on the pasta and toss well. Keep aside.

2. For the sauce, heat oil. Add garlic and ginger. Stir. Add tomato puree and cook for about 15 minutes till oil separates.

3. Add all masalas, baby corn and fenugreek leaves. Cook on low heat for 5 minutes.

4. Add cashew paste and mix well. Cook on low heat till thick and dry.

5. Add 1 cup reserved pasta water and bring to a boil. Simmer on low heat for 3-4 minutes. Remove from heat. Let it cool down to room temperature.

6. To serve, add cream, milk and pasta to the gravy and mix well. Heat well on low fire. Serve hot.

Fish Fusilli Pescatore

Ingredients for this recipe can easily be doubled up to serve six.
Why not try it with plenty of garlic bread and green salad.

Serves 3

200 gm boneless fish - cut into 1" square pieces
1 tsp dry parsley or oregano
2 tbsp oil, preferably olive oil
1 tsp crushed garlic, 1 onion - finely chopped (½ cup)
1 small capsicum - finely chopped (½ cup)
2 tomatoes - blanched and finely chopped
1 cup tomato puree
¼ cup white wine (optional)
1 cup water, 1 tsp salt (or to taste), ¾ tsp pepper (or to taste)
2 tbsp chopped fresh parsley or coriander, ½ tsp sugar

TO SERVE
(1½ cups) raw pasta (*fusilli*)
1-2 tsp oil and 1 tbsp chopped parsley or oregano

1. Boil pasta, boil 8-10 cups of water in a large pan. Add 2 tsp salt and 1 tbsp oil. Drop the pasta to boiling water. Boil for 7-8 minutes or till the pasta turns soft but is still firm. Remove from fire and let the pasta stay in hot water for 2-3 minutes. Strain reserving the water. Refresh in cold water and strain again. Leave pasta in strainer for 15 minutes so that all the water drains out. Sprinkle 1-2 tbsp olive oil and 1 tsp dried parsley or oregano on the pasta and toss well. Keep aside.

2. To blanch tomatoes, keep them in hot water for 10 minutes. Peel and chop finely.

3. Heat oil. Add fish and cook till brown and cooked. Remove fish from pan.

4. In the same oil add garlic. Fry for 1 minute.

5. Add onion and capsicum and fry till light pink.

6. Add chopped tomatoes, tomato puree, wine, salt and pepper. Mix well.

7. Add wine or 1 cup reserved pasta water. Mix well. Cover and cook on low heat for 10 minutes.

8. Add fish, parsley and sugar. Mix well. Check salt and pepper and keep on fire till properly heated.

9. Serve boiled pasta on the side with the fish mixture. Garnish with lemon wedges and sprigs of parsley.

Zucchini and Mushroom Pasta

This dish is easy to prepare and makes a very healthy and satisfying meal.

Serves 4

2 cups rigatoni pasta or any other pasta
2 tbsp olive oil, 2 onions - chopped
200 gm mushrooms (10-12) - sliced
1 zucchini (*tori*) - thinly sliced (2 cups)
6 tomatoes, 2 tbsp tomato puree or 1½ tbsp tomato ketchup
2 tbsp chopped fresh basil or parsley or coriander
2 bay leaves (*tej patta*)
2 tbsp grated cheddar cheese
½ tsp pepper
1 veg seasoning soup cube - crushed
2 tbsp cream to garnish

1. Boil 8-10 cups of water in a large pan. Add 2 tsp salt and 1 tbsp oil. Drop the pasta in boiling water. Boil for 7-8 minutes or till pasta turns soft but is still firm. Remove from fire and let the pasta stay in hot water for 2-3 minutes. Strain. Refresh in cold water and strain again. Leave pasta in strainer for 15 minutes so that all the water drains out. Sprinkle 1-2 tbsp olive oil on the pasta and toss well. Keep aside.

2. To blanch tomatoes, boil whole tomatoes in water for 3-4 minutes, or till soft. Drain. Cool. Peel and chop the blanched tomatoes.

3. Heat oil in a saucepan, add onions, stir over moderate heat until tender for about 3-4 minutes.

4. Add mushrooms and zuchhini. Cook for 5-7 minutes.

5. Add tomatoes, tomato puree, basil and bay leaves. Bring to a boil, cover, reduce heat and let it, simmer for 10 minutes or until sauce has reduced and thickened.

6. Add pepper and seasoning soup cube. Mix well. Check seasonings. Remove from fire. Remove bay leaf.

7. To serve, heat sauce in a pan, add pasta and mix well.

8. To serve pour pasta in a serving dish and swirl with cream. Garnish with fresh herbs, if desired.

Baked Veg Bolognese

The Bolognese sauce made vegetarian, substituting minced meat with Soy granules.

Serves 6-8

3 cups (200 gm) penne - boiled (5 cups)

VEGETARIAN BOLOGNESE SAUCE

2 cups (100 gm) Soy granules - soaked in 4 cups of water for 1 hour or more

1 capsicum - cut into ½" pieces, 1 tsp crushed garlic or paste

1 large onion - chopped fine (1 cup), 1 tbsp chopped celery stalks, optional

400 gm (5 medium) tomatoes - churn in mixer for puree

1 tsp dry basil & 1 tsp dry oregano or 2 tsp mixed herbs, 2 tsp salt, ½ tsp pepper

½ tsp red chilli powder, 1 tbsp chopped fresh parsley or coriander

½ cup red wine or water, 3 tbsp olive oil or any cooking oil

WHITE SAUCE

2½ tbsp softened butter, 2½ tbsp plain flour (*maida*), 2½ cups milk

100 gms cheese - grated (1 cup), ½ tsp freshly ground black pepper, ¾ tsp salt, or to taste

1. Boil 7 cups of water with 1 tsp of salt and oil. Drop pasta in boiling water and cook for 8 minutes or till soft. Remove. Strain. Put in cold water to refresh & strain again. Coat with 1 tbsp oil.

2. To prepare the sauce, heat 3 tbsp oil in a kadhai. Add garlic, onion and celery and cook till well browned.

3. Drain granules and squeeze well. Add Soy granules to onions and cook for 5-7 minutes on moderate heat till they brown well.

4. Add basil, oregano, salt, pepper and red chilli powder. Mix. Add pureed tomatoes and ½ cup water. Cook for 10 minutes till oil separates. Add parsley, ½ cup wine or water. Bring to a boil. Remove from fire.

5. Add boiled penne to the sauce. Toss well and spread in a greased baking dish.

6. For white sauce, heat butter in a heavy saucepan or kadhai over low heat and stir in black pepper, and flour and saute for about 1 minute. Remove from heat.

7. Gradually pour milk, stirring continuously until the sauce is smooth. Cook for 2 minutes, till it starts coating the spoon and turns a little thick. Add salt. Remove from fire. Cool slightly.

8. Add ½ cup cheese to the white sauce. Pour the sauce over the pasta in the baking dish. Cover with the left over cheese. Cover with aluminium foil. Bake for about 20 minutes at 180°C/350°F till golden and bubbling. Serve hot with garlic bread.

Roasted Tomato Pasta

The sweetness of tomatoes is brought out by roasting them –
the secret of the success of this classic dish.

Serves 5-6

450 gm penne or fusilli pasta, 2 tbsp olive oil
1 onion - thinly sliced, 5 mushrooms - sliced
¼ cup corn kernels, ¼ cup chopped red or green capsicum
1 tbsp sliced black olives, 1 tsp red chilli flakes, 2 tsp dried or fresh basil

SAUCE
1 kg tomatoes - cut into ½" thick slices
10 flakes of garlic with the peel, 3 tbsp fresh orange juice, 1½ tsp dried oregano
1½ tsp salt, 1 tsp pepper, 3 tbsp tomato ketchup, 2 tbsp cream (optional)

1. Boil 8-10 cups of water in a large pan. Add 2 tsp salt and 1 tbsp oil. Drop pasta in boiling water. Boil for 7-8 minutes or till pasta turns soft but is still firm. Remove from fire and let the pasta stay in hot water for 2-3 minutes. Strain. Refresh in cold water and strain again. Leave pasta in strainer for 15 minutes so that all the water drains out. Sprinkle 1-2 tbsp olive oil on the pasta and toss well. Keep aside.

2. Preheat oven to 220°C. Lightly brush baking tray with oil.

3. Arrange tomato slices in one single layer on the baking tray or cover the wire rack of the oven with aluminium foil and place the tomatoes on it.

4. Sprinkle ½ tsp of oregano, a little salt and pepper over the tomatoes.

5. Wrap all garlic flakes together in a piece of foil. Seal tightly.

6. Place wrapped garlic along with the tomatoes. Roast garlic & tomatoes in the preheated oven for about 30 minutes.

7. Unwrap garlic and cool slightly. Peel.

8. Blend the roasted tomatoes, garlic, oregano, orange juice, salt, pepper, tomato ketchup and cream to a smooth puree. Keep aside.

9. Heat 2 tbsp olive oil in a large pan. Add onion and saute till soft. Add mushrooms. Cook for a minute. Add the prepared tomato sauce. Mix.

10. Add the boiled pasta, corn, capsicum, black olives, chilli flakes and basil. Check salt and pepper. Serve hot.

Pasta in Quick Tomato Sauce

Any easy recipe to make, this simple pasta is delicious to eat.

Serves 4

3 cups penne or any other pasta
2 medium green or coloured capsicums, 2 medium tomatoes
1 tbsp oil, 2 tsp crushed garlic, 1 cup ready-made tomato puree
¾ tsp pepper, 1 tsp oregano, 1½ tsp salt, 1¼ cups milk, ½ cup cream (optional)

1. Boil 8-10 cups of water in a large pan. Add 2 tsp salt and 1 tbsp oil. Drop pasta in boiling water. Boil for 7-8 minutes or till pasta turns soft but is still firm. Remove from fire and let the pasta stay in hot water for 2-3 minutes. Strain. Refresh in cold water and strain again. Leave pasta in strainer for 15 minutes so that all the water drains out. Sprinkle 1-2 tbsp olive oil on the pasta and toss well. Keep aside.

2. Cut tomatoes into 4 pieces. Remove pulp. Cut into thin long fingers. Cut capsicum also into thin long fingers.

3. Heat 1 tbsp oil in a wok, add ½ tsp garlic, saute for ½ minute. Add boiled pasta, saute for 1-2 minutes. Add ¼ tsp pepper and ½ tsp oregano. Toss, remove pasta from the wok.

4. In the same wok heat 3 tbsp oil. Add 1½ tsp crushed garlic. Stir till it changes colour.

5. Add 1 cup ready-made tomato puree. Cook for 3-4 minutes or till oil separates.

6. Add ½ tsp pepper, ½ tsp oregano and 1½ tsp salt. Mix. Reduce heat and cook for 2 minutes. Add boiled pasta, toss well. Keep aside.

7. At serving time, heat the pasta on fire. Add capsicum, tomato, milk and cream. Toss well. Check salt and pepper. Remove from fire. Serve hot with garlic bread.

fresh puree
(1 cup)

ready-made
puree (½ cup)

3 tomatoes gives 1 cup fresh puree

TiP

For fresh tomato puree: Tomatoes are roughly chopped and ground to a puree in a mixer-grinder. Instead of using raw tomatoes they are sometimes blanched.

You can also add cream to this dish. If using cream then add 1 cup milk and ½ cup cream to this dish.

If you have any other pasta shape at home e.g macaroni, rigatoni etc., use it instead of penne.

Spaghetti Bolognese

A favourite with youngsters and adults. Enjoy the subtle seasoning of oregano and basil.

Serves 3-4

450 gm mutton or chicken mince *(keema),* 300 gm spaghetti - boiled (given below)
4 tbsp olive oil, 1 onion - chopped, 2 flakes garlic - chopped, 8 tomatoes
8 fresh basil leaves, 1 tsp dried oregano, ¼ cup grated pizza cheese
1 tsp salt, ½ tsp freshly ground black pepper

1. Blanch whole tomatoes in boiling water for 3-4 minutes. Remove from water. Peel the tomatoes and puree in a mixer. Keep tomato puree aside.

2. Heat olive oil in a large pan. Add the onion and garlic. Saute over medium heat until the onions become very soft for about 8 minutes.

3. Add chicken mince. Saute on high heat stirring frequently and breaking large lumps, if any. Cook for about 8 minutes and not more or the mince will lose its red colour.

4. Add the tomatoes, basil & oregano. Cook over medium heat until the sauce thickens and the chicken mince is cooked (about ½ hour).

5. Add cheese, salt and pepper. Check seasonings. Keep sauce aside.

6. To serve, arrange boiled spaghetti in a serving dish. Pour the prepared Bolognese sauce over the cooked spaghetti. Toss. Serve hot.

How to boil spaghetti/fettuccine

Boil 8-10 cups of water (½ of a big pan).

Add 2 tsp salt & 1 tbsp oil. Holding the bunch of spaghetti/fettuccine, start slipping it from the side into the water. As it softens, all the spaghetti easily fits into the pan.

Stir at intervals to check that it does not stick to the bottom of the pan. Boil, stirring occasionally, for about 7-8 minutes till it turns almost soft, but yet firm. Do not overcook. Remove from fire and leave it in hot water for 2-3 minutes. Strain. Leave for 5 minutes in the strainer for the water to drain. Spoon 1 tbsp olive oil on cooked spaghetti to prevent it from sticking. Toss gently. Use when required.

Macaroni in Arabiatta Sauce

Make this popular red sauce and add the pasta to it at serving time.

Serves 4

2½ cups macaroni or any other pasta - (about 4 cups when boiled)
½ of a small flower of broccoli - cut into small florets (1 cup florets)

SAUCE

2 tbsp olive oil or butter, 1 small onion - very finely chopped, 2 garlic flakes - crushed
500 gm tomatoes
½ cup ready-made tomato puree, ½ cup chopped fresh parsley, 2 tbsp chopped celery
½ of a small green or yellow or red capsicum - chopped, 1 tsp dried oregano
1 tbsp tomato sauce, 1 tsp sugar, 1¼ tsp salt
¼ tsp freshly ground pepper, some red chilli flakes, ½ cup milk

1. To boil pasta, see page 10.

2. Cut broccoli into very small florets with little or no stalk, (about 1 cup chopped). Boil 4 cups water with 1 tsp salt and 1 tsp sugar. Add broccoli and remove from heat. Leave broccoli in hot water for 2 minutes. Remove broccoli with a slotted spoon. Refresh in cold water. Strain and wipe dry on a clean kitchen towel.

3. Blanch the tomatoes by boiling in water for 3-4 minutes. Remove from water. Peel them and puree in a mixer. Sieve the puree.

4. For the sauce, heat 2 tbsp oil. Add onions and garlic, cook until onions turn light brown. Add ¼ cup parsley & stir for 1 minute. Add chopped celery & green capsicum.

5. Add fresh and ready-made tomato puree, oregano, tomato sauce, salt, pepper and sugar. Add red chilli flakes to taste. Cook for 5 minutes on low heat, stirring occasionally till a little thick. Add the remaining parsley. Cook for 1-2 minutes more. Remove from heat and let it cool down slightly.

6. Add milk stirring continuously. Keep sauce aside.

7. To serve, heat sauce, add pasta with broccoli. Toss well. Remove from heat. Transfer to a serving platter. Serve hot, topped with some grated cheese, if desired.

PASTA IN CREAMY SAUCES

Macaroni Cheese

Children's favourite! You can vary this popular family favourite by adding chopped ham, chopped red or green peppers, finely chopped onion or chopped fresh parsley to the sauce.

Serves 6

315 gm or 3¼ cup macaroni - boiled
¼ cup grated cheddar cheese

CHEESE SAUCE
5 tbsp butter, 5 tbsp flour (*maida*), 1 tsp dry mustard powder
2½ cups milk, ½ cup grated cheddar cheese
½ tsp freshly ground black pepper

1. To boil pasta, see page 10.

2. To make sauce, melt butter in a saucepan over medium heat. Stir in flour & mustard. Cook, stirring, for 1 minute. Remove pan from heat and whisk in milk. Return pan to heat and cook, stirring, for 5-6 minutes or until sauce boils and thickens. Stir in cheese and black pepper to taste.

3. Pour sauce over pasta, sprinkle with cheese and bake for 20-25 minutes at 180°C, or until hot and bubbling with a golden layer on top.

Twists in Ham Broccoli Sauce

Rich, creamy and satisfying, this is a comforting dish to serve when it's cold outside.

Serves 3

150 gm chicken or pork ham - diced (keep aside some for garnishing)
2½ cups serpentine pasta - boiled
250 gm broccoli - half grated and half cut into tiny florets
3 tbsp butter, ¾ cup chopped onion
1 tsp crushed garlic, 2¼ tbsp flour (*maida*)
2 cups milk or 1½ cups milk+½ cup cream
a pinch of nutmeg (*jaiphal*), ½ tsp salt
½ tsp pepper, 1 tsp oregano

1. To boil pasta, boil 8-10 cups of water in a large pan. Add 2 tsp salt and 1 tbsp oil. Add the pasta to the boiling water. Boil for 7-8 minutes or till pasta turn soft but is still firm. Remove from fire and let the pasta be in hot water for 2-3 minutes. Strain. Refresh in cold water and strain again. Leave pasta in strainer for 15 minutes so that all the water drains out. Sprinkle 1-2 tbsp olive oil on the pasta and mix well. Keep aside.

2. Grate half of the broccoli and cut half into tiny florets with a little stem.

3. Boil 1 cup water. Drop broccoli florets in it and cook for 2 minutes. Strain. Remove with slotted spoon.

4. Add grated broccoli to boiling water and cook for 2-3 minutes. Strain.

5. Heat 3 tbsp butter in a pan, add onion and garlic. Cook over medium heat until onion is translucent.

6. Add grated broccoli. Cook for 2 minutes.

7. Add flour, cook for a minute, stirring.

8. Pour milk stirring continuously with one hand. Increase heat to medium; cook 3 minutes longer or until sauce is thick and creamy.

9. Add ham, nutmeg, salt, pepper and oregano. Check seasonings. Remove from fire.

10. Toss pasta in a pan with 1 tbsp butter and ½ tsp oregano. Mix well.

11. To serve, arrange hot pasta in a plate. Pour sauce in the centre. Garnish with a few ham strips.

Pasta in Garlic Butter Sauce

Try something different!

Serves 4

3 cups shell pasta or any other pasta

½ tsp salt, ½ tsp sugar, 1 tbsp coriander - chopped

SAUCE

¾ cup vegetable stock or 1 veg seasoning soup cube (Maggi or Knorr), 3 tbsp butter

3 spring onions (*hara pyaz*) - chopped with the greens

15 flakes garlic - crushed to a paste (1 tbsp)

1 tbsp chopped coriander, 3½ tbsp flour (*maida*), 1 cup milk

2 tsp mustard paste (optional), ½ tsp pepper, ½ tsp salt, or to taste

1 cup thin cream (if the cream is thick, then thin it down with ¼ cup milk and then measure to get 1 cup thin cream)

1. Boil 8-10 cups of water in a large pan. Add 2 tsp salt and 1 tbsp oil. Drop pasta in boiling water. Boil for 7-8 minutes or till pasta turns soft but is still firm. Remove from fire and let the pasta stay in hot water for 2-3 minutes. Strain. Refresh in cold water and strain again. Leave pasta in strainer for 15 minutes so that all the water drains out. Sprinkle 1-2 tbsp olive oil on the pasta and toss mix well. Keep aside.

2. To make stock with cube, boil 1 cup water with 1 seasoning soup cube. Give one boil and remove from fire. Keep aside.

3. In a heavy bottom pan put 3 tbsp butter. Add white of onions and cook till soft.

4. Add garlic paste. Cook till garlic changes colour.

5. Add coriander, stir fry for 2 minutes.

6. Add flour. Stir for 1 minute on medium flame till light golden.

7. Reduce heat. Add milk, stirring continuously.

8. Add prepared stock, mustard paste, pepper and salt. Cook stirring, on low flame till sauce thickens. Remove from fire.

9. Add cream and green of spring onions. Keep aside till serving time.

10. At serving time, heat sauce on low heat, add boiled pasta, toss gently. Serve hot.

50

Traditional Lasagne

Serves 4

6 lasagne sheets
1 cup grated mozzarella or pizza cheese

CHEESE SAUCE
3 tbsp butter, 2 tbsp flour (*maida*), 1½ cup milk, ½ cup grated cheddar cheese
½ tsp freshly ground pepper, ¾ tsp salt, 3 tsp chopped parsley or coriander

MEAT SAUCE
½ kg mutton mince (*keema*), 4 tbsp oil, 2 onions-chopped, 1 tsp crushed garlic, ½ kg tomatoes
¾ cup red wine (optional), 2 tbsp oregano, ½ tsp pepper, ½ tsp red chilli flakes, 1 tsp salt

1. To make cheese sauce, melt butter in a saucepan over medium heat. Stir in flour. Cook, stirring, for 1 minute. Remove pan from heat and whisk in milk. Return pan to heat and cook, stirring, for 4-5 minutes or until sauce boils and thickens. Stir in cheese, pepper, salt and parsley. Keep aside.

2. Boil whole tomatoes in water for 3-4 minutes, or till soft. Drain. Cool. Peel and chop the blanched tomatoes.

3. To make meat sauce, heat oil in a pressure cooker. Add onions and garlic and cook, stirring, for 3 minutes or until onions are soft. Add mince and cook, stirring, for 10 minutes. Add blanched tomatoes, puree, wine, oregano, pepper, red chilli flakes and salt. Bring to a boil. Cover with lid and allow one whistle. Reduce heat and cook on low heat for 5 minutes. Let the pressure drop by itself. Check seasonings.

4. Wet lasagne sheets by dipping in water. Line the base of a greased baking dish with 2 wet lasagne sheets. Leave space all around sheets and also in between sheets. Spread with some cheese sauce, cover with tomato mince, sprinkle cheese. Cover with another layer of wet lasagne sheets. Repeat using up all the prepared sauces and lasagne sheets in the same way. Cover the last sheet with cheese sauce completely.

5. Sprinkle the top with mozzarella cheese. Cover lightly with foil.

6. Bake for 45 minutes at 180°C/350°F/gas 4 or until hot and bubbling with a golden top layer. Remove cover and bake for another 5 minutes. Serve hot.

TiP

Lasagne goes well with a salad of mixed vegetables tossed in an Italian dressing.

Thai Basil Pasta

For coconut lovers! My personal favourite for the summer weather!

Serves 2

150 gm spaghetti - boiled (2 cups)

3 tomatoes - blanched

2 tbsp olive oil

1 tsp crushed garlic

1 cup ready-made coconut milk

1 tsp grated lemon peel or 2-3 lemon leaves-shredded

1 tsp salt

1 tsp ground black pepper

¼ - ½ cup chopped fresh basil leaves - roughly torn with hands

1. Boil 8-10 cups of water (½ of a big pan). Add 2 tsp salt and 1 tbsp oil. Holding the bunch of spaghetti, start slipping it from the side into the water. As it softens, all the spaghetti easily fits into the pan. Stir in-between to check that it does not stick to the bottom of the pan. Boil, stirring occasionally, for about 7-8 minutes till it turns almost soft, but yet firm. Do not overcook. Remove from fire and leave in hot water for 2-3 minutes till done. Strain. Leave for 5 minutes in the strainer for the water to drain. Spoon 1 tbsp olive oil on cooked spaghetti to prevent it from sticking. Toss gently. Use when required.

2. To blanch tomatoes, bring 4 cups of water to a boil in a saucepan. Drop the tomatoes, in the boiling water for 3-4 minutes, to loosen the skin. Peel skins from boiled tomatoes. Chop the peeled tomatoes. Discard skins.

3. In a pan, heat oil, add tomatoes and garlic to hot oil and stir constantly until most of the liquid has evaporated and mixture is reduced to half.

4. Add coconut milk, lemon peel, salt and pepper. Simmer gently for 2 minutes until sauce is heated well and flavours have blended.

5. Add spaghetti, toss well. Serve hot.

TiP

To make the work simpler, boil 8-10 cups of water. Add tomatoes. Boil for 3-4 minutes. Remove tomatoes from water. Boil spaghetti in the same water.

Penne & Prawns in Saffron Sauce

Delicious prawns, with a saffron flavoured pasta sauce.

Serves 2

2 cups shell pasta or any other pasta
250 gm medium sized prawns - shelled and deveined, or 250 gm frozen shrimps - thawed
½ cup boiled peas (*matar*)

SAFFRON SAUCE
4 tbsp butter
2 tbsp flour (*maida*)
1 cup milk
¼ tsp saffron threads or a pinch of saffron (*kesar*) powder
1 tsp dried sage or oregano
½ tsp salt

1. Boil 8-10 cups of water in a large pan. Add 2 tsp salt and 1 tbsp oil. Drop pasta in boiling water. Boil for 7-8 minutes or till pasta turns soft but is still firm. Remove from fire and let the pasta stay in hot water for 2-3 minutes. Strain. Refresh in cold water and strain again. Leave pasta in strainer for 15 minutes so that all the water drains out. Sprinkle 1-2 tbsp olive oil on the pasta and toss well. Keep aside.

2. To make sauce, melt butter in a small saucepan over medium heat, add prawns or shrimps and stir fry for 2- 3 minutes. Add flour and cook for 1 minute. Remove pan from heat and whisk in milk, saffron and sage. Return pan to heat and cook, stirring, for 5 minutes or until sauce boils and thickens.

3. Add peas and salt, mix. Keep aside till serving time.

4. At serving time add pasta and toss. Check seasonings. Serve hot.

TiP

Although saffron is an expensive spice, here you require a little to add wonderful colour and flavour to food. Food flavoured with saffron has a distinct aroma, a bitter honey-like taste and strong yellow colour.

Bow with Walnut Sauce

An appetizing mixture of pasta in a walnut sauce.

Serves 2

1½ cups bow pasta or any other pasta

WALNUT SAUCE

¼ cup walnuts (*akhrot*)

½ cup fresh basil leaves (stems discarded) or mint leaves (*poodina*)

2 tbsp butter

1 onion - chopped

1 tomato - cut into 4 long pieces, remove center pulp and slice

¼ cup thin cream

4 tbsp grated cheddar cheese (optional)

¼ cup cream or milk

½ tsp freshly ground black pepper

½ tsp salt or to taste

1. Boil 8-10 cups of water in a large pan. Add 2 tsp salt and 1 tbsp oil. Drop pasta in boiling water. Boil for 7-8 minutes or till the pasta turns soft but is still firm. Remove from fire and let the pasta stay in hot water for 2-3 minutes. Strain. Refresh in cold water and strain again. Leave pasta in strainer for 15 minutes so that all the water drains out. Sprinkle 1-2 tbsp olive oil on the pasta and toss well. Keep aside.

2. Put walnuts and basil in a food processor or blender and chop fine.

3. Heat butter in a pan, add onion, cook till soft.

4. Add black pepper and salt to taste.

5. Add walnut paste, cream, milk, tomato & cheese. Mix well. Keep aside till serving time.

6. At serving time heat sauce, add pasta. Add a little milk for about 4 tbsp if pasta turns dry. Mix well. Serve hot.

TiP

Take care while churning walnuts with basil. Process it briefly or until the two are just combined. If you over process the flavour would be gone.

Chicken Parmagiana with Linguine

Crispy chicken breast served with pasta. For a bigger group slice the fried breast into slices and top over hot pasta.

Serves 4

10-12 bunches of linguine pasta or 300 gms spaghetti
2 boneless chicken breasts (225 gms) - cut each breast horizontally into two pieces
1 cup cornflakes - roughly crushed

MARINADE
1 egg (use only white portion), 1 tsp minced garlic
¾ tsp salt, ½ tsp pepper, 1 tbsp oil

SAUCE
3 tbsp butter, 7-8 spring onions (*hara pyaz*) - chopped with the greens, 4 tbsp flour (*maida*)
1 seasoning cube (soup cube) - crushed, 1 cup milk
¾ tsp freshly ground pepper to taste, 4 tbsp grated cheese (optional)

1. Boil 8-10 cups of water in a large pan. Add 2 tsp salt and 1 tbsp oil. Drop pasta in boiling water. Boil for 7-8 minutes or till pasta turns soft but is still firm. Remove from fire and let the pasta stay in hot water for 2-3 minutes. Strain. Refresh in cold water and strain again. Leave pasta in strainer for 15 minutes so that all the water drains out. Sprinkle 1-2 tbsp olive oil on the pasta and toss well. Keep aside.

2. Mix all ingredients of the marinade in a bowl. Put chicken breasts and coat on all sides with the marinade. Keep aside to marinate for 1 hour or more.

3. Spread cornflakes in a plate, pick up the chicken breast from the marinade and coat on all sides with cornflakes.

4. Heat 6 tbsp oil in a pan, add chicken breast and pan fry on medium heat till golden and cooked on both sides. Keep aside.

5. Melt butter in a pan over medium-low heat, add white of the onions, cook till onions turn soft. Add flour, mix well.

6. Stirring continuously add stock cube, milk and 3 cups reserved pasta water. Increase heat and cook stirring until the sauce reduces to a thick sauce.

7. Add greens of spring onions and pasta, toss well. Check seasonings.

8. Serve pasta with the hot chicken breast on the side. Offer the cheese separately.

Shrimps in Creamy Mushroom Sauce

Serve it with fresh crusty bread.

Serves 2

1½ cup penne pasta

250 gms frozen shrimps - thawed

100 gms mushrooms or 100 gms babycorns - sliced

2 tbsp butter

2 tbsp flour

1 tsp crushed garlic

1 onion - chopped

½ tsp pepper

¼ tsp salt

1 stock soup cube

1 cup milk

½ cup cream

¼ cup basil - roughly torn with hands

a dash of tabasco

4 tbsp grated cheddar cheese

1. Boil 8-10 cups of water in a large pan. Add 2 tsp salt and 1 tbsp oil. Drop pasta in boiling water. Boil for 7-8 minutes or till pasta turns soft but is still firm. Remove from fire and let the pasta stay in hot water for 2-3 minutes. Strain. Refresh in cold water and strain again. Leave pasta in strainer for 15 minutes so that all the water drains out. Sprinkle 1-2 tbsp olive oil on the pasta and toss well. Keep aside.

2. Melt butter in pan, add onion and cook till soft. Add garlic, cook for a minute, add mushrooms and cook on high flame till mushrooms dry out completely for about 5-6 minutes.

3. Add shrimps, stir for 2 minutes.

4. Add flour, salt, pepper, stock cube, milk, cream, basil, tabasco and cheese. Cook until mixture boils and thickens, stirring constantly.

5. Add pasta. Toss well. Serve hot.

Chicken Cannelloni

Tubes of pasta filled with chicken and baked!

Serves 4

7 cannelloni tubes

WHITE SAUCE
2 tbsp butter, 2 tbsp flour, 1 cup milk,
½ cup reserved pasta water, 1½ tbsp garlic
½ tsp freshly ground black pepper
½ tsp salt, 1 tsp oregano

FILLING
375 gms chicken mince (*keema*), 3 tbsp oil, 1½ onions - chopped
½ tsp crushed garlic, a pinch of cinnamon (*dalchini*) powder
½ tsp red chilli flakes, ½ tsp bhuna jeera powder
1 tsp salt, 2 tbsp ketchup, 4 tbsp cheddar cheese, ½ tsp pepper

1. Boil ready made cannelloni tubes in 8 cups boiling water with 1 tsp salt and 1 tbsp oil for 5-6 minutes till soft, yet firm. Reserve ½ cup of pasta water. Remove on a well greased aluminium foil. Make sure that they do not overlap. Cover with a cling flim.

2. To make white sauce, melt butter in a saucepan over a medium heat. Add garlic cook for few seconds. Stir in flour and cook, stirring, for 1 minute. Remove pan from heat and whisk in milk. Return pan to heat, add ½ cup reserved pasta water and cook, stirring, for 4–5 minutes or until sauce boils and thickens. Add black pepper, salt and oregano. Keep aside.

3. To make filling, heat oil in a pan. Add onions & garlic and cook, stirring, for 3 minutes or until onions are soft. Add mince and cook, stirring, for 5- 7 minutes. Add dalchini powder, red chilli flakes, bhuna jeera powder, salt, ketchup and pepper. Cook covered for 3-4 minutes or till chicken is cooked. Add cheese. Mix. Check seasonings Remove from fire.

4. Stuff tubes with the prepared filling.

5. Spread 2 tbsp sauce on the base of a baking dish. Arrange tubes on sauce. Pour sauce on top. Sprinkle chopped coriander or parsley. Cover lightly with foil.

6. Bake for 20 minutes at 180°C/350°F/gas 4 or until hot and bubbling with the top layer golden.

Peanut Sauce Penne

Pasta in peanut sauce. A new invention for the peanut lovers.

Serves 4

2 cups penne pasta
5 tbsp ready-made peanut butter
½ cup water or vegetable stock
2 tbsp soy sauce
1 tbsp white-wine vinegar or rice vinegar
1 tsp honey or rice syrup
¼ tsp ground ginger (*saunth*)
½ tsp salt
½ tsp red chilli powder or flakes
1 tbsp butter

1. Boil 8-10 cups of water in a large pan. Add 2 tsp salt and 1 tbsp oil. Drop pasta in boiling water. Boil for 7-8 minutes or till pasta turns soft but is still firm. Remove from fire and let the pasta stay in hot water for 2-3 minutes. Strain. Refresh in cold water and strain again. Leave pasta in strainer for 15 minutes so that all the water drains out. Sprinkle 1-2 tbsp olive oil on the pasta and toss well. Keep aside.

2. Combine peanut butter, water, soy sauce, vinegar, honey, ginger, salt and chilli powder in a mixer. Process until smooth.

3. Heat butter in a pan, add peanut sauce and boiled pasta. Mix well. Server hot.

TiP

The peanut butter sauce thickens as it stands. Mix in more water if the dish sits for a while before serving, or is served as a leftover the next day.

Spinach Pasta in Carbonara Sauce

Carbonara, in Italian cooking is a sauce with eggs. The eggs get cooked when poured over very hot pasta. Spinach is kneaded into pasta dough to make green-coloured pasta. It is available at large grocey stores.

Serves 4

200 gm green spinach pasta
1 tbsp olive oil
2 eggs
1 cup grated cheddar cheese, ½ cup cream
2 tbsp butter
1¼ tsp minced garlic, 1 onion - sliced (½ cup)
½ cup frozen peas (*matar*)
1 tsp oregano, salt and pepper to taste

1. Lightly beat eggs in a bowl. Add cream and cheese and keep aside.

2. Heat butter in a pan. Add minced garlic. Stir. Add onion. Saute for 7-8 minutes till light golden. Add peas. Keep aside till pasta is boiled.

3. Boil 8-10 cups of water in a large pan. Add 2 tsp salt and 1 tbsp oil. Drop pasta in boiling water. Boil for 7-8 minutes or till pasta turns soft but is still firm. Remove from fire and let the pasta stay in hot water for 2-3 minutes. Strain. Sprinkle 1-2 tbsp olive oil on the pasta and toss well.

4. Transfer pasta to a large mixing bowl. Immediately add beaten egg mixture to the hot pasta, slowly in a stream, mixing with the other hand. Mix well. The eggs get cooked in the heat of the pasta. Add onion, peas, salt, pepper and oregano. Toss well. Serve hot.

Gnocchi with Tomato Cream Sauce

Light as air, delicate as a flower – and easy to make!

Serves 2

GNOCCHI
3 potatoes - boiled, cooled & grated finely (1¼ cups)
1 tbsp butter
2 tbsp flour (*maida*)
1 tbsp chopped basil or parsley
½ tsp salt
½ tsp pepper

SAUCE
¼ cup cream, ¼ cup milk
¼ tsp salt
½ tsp freshly ground black pepper
2 tomatoes - chopped

1. Boil the potatoes. Wipe the boiled potatoes and let them air dry. Peel and grate finely.

2. Add butter, maida, salt, pepper and basil/parsley to the potatoes. Mix and knead well for about 5-6 minutes.

3. Lightly dust the working surface with maida.

4. Take a portion of the mixture and roll into a sausage. Using a knife cut into ½" long pieces. Make a ball and flatten it with the thumb to get a slight depression. Repeat with the rest of the mixture.

5. Boil 10 cups of water with ½ tsp salt in a big pan.

6. Add the prepared gnocchi. Let it float on the water. Cook gnocchi for another 30 seconds from the time it rises to the surface.

7. Remove the cooked gnocchi with a slotted spoon. Keep aside.

8. For the sauce, mix cream and milk in a heavy-bottomed saucepan. Bring to a boil.

9. Add salt and pepper to taste.

10. Gently stir in tomatoes. Cook for a minute.

11. Add gnocchi. Cook to thicken the cream. Remove from fire. Serve hot.

Fettuccine with Pumpkin

The combination of sweet butternut pumpkin, chives and sharp nutmeg works wonderfully for fettuccine.

Serves 2

6 bunches of coiled green fettuccine or 2 cups fettuccine - boiled

1½ cups chopped pumpkin (*kaddu*)

4 tbsp butter

1 tsp garlic

1 tsp oregano

¾ cup milk

3 tbsp cream

1 big onion - sliced

¼ tsp freshly ground black pepper

½ tsp ground nutmeg (*jaiphal*)

3 tbsp snipped chives or coriander or parsley

½ tsp red chilli flakes, salt to taste

1. To boil fettuccine, see page 42.

2. Heat 2 tbsp butter in a pan. Add all the chopped pumpkin. Pan fry till golden on all sides. Sprinkle oregano. Keep aside.

3. Keep aside ½ cup chopped pumpkin and puree the remaining in a mixer.

4. Heat 2 tbsp butter, garlic and onion. Cook till onion gets golden. Add pureed pumpkin.

5. Add milk, cream, parsley, chilli flakes, nutmeg and salt.

6. Add fettuccine and toss gently till heated well.

7. Serve topped with golden fried pumpkin cubes (see picture).

Herb Tortellini in Cream Cheese Sauce

Herb tortellini stuffed with cheese and tossed with vegetables in garlic butter.

Serves 4

HERB TORTELLINI
1 cup plain flour (*maida*), 1 tsp dried oregano
1 tsp chopped parsley
1 tsp red chilli flakes, 4 tbsp olive oil
½ tsp salt to taste

FILLING
½ cup grated broccoli
½ cup very thinly sliced babycorn
2 tbsp grated cheese
½ tsp salt, ¼ tsp pepper

SAUCE
2 tbsp butter, 3 tbsp plain flour (*maida*)
3 - 4 mushrooms - finely chopped
½ onion - chopped, 1 cup milk
¼ cup water
1 tbsp chopped parsley or fresh coriander
½ tsp salt, or to taste
¼ tsp pepper or to taste
2- 3 tbsp grated cheese
½ cup cream

1. Mix all ingredients of the filling in a bowl. Keep aside.

2. For the tortellini, sieve the flour and salt together.

3. Add the oregano, parsley, chilli flakes and olive oil and knead to a firm dough adding a little cold water if necessary.

4. Cover with a wet muslin cloth and allow it to rest for about 15 minutes.

5. Divide the dough into two portions and roll out each portion as thinly as you can without breaking the sheet.

6. Using a 2" diameter cookie cutter, cut the sheet into circles.

Contd...

7. Place ½ tsp of the filling in little heaps in the centre of each circle.

8. Brush the sides of the circle with a little cold water and fold it into a semicircle sealing the edges.

9. Brush the corners of the semicircle with cold water and join them together by pressing the edges firmly.

10. Cook the tortellini for 5- 6 minutes in a large pan of boiling water to which 1 tsp of salt and 1 tbsp of oil has been added.

11. Drain and transfer the herb tortellini into a bowl of cold water. Drain again.

12. Sprinkle 1 tbsp oil and mix gently. Keep aside till serving time.

13. To prepare the sauce, heat butter. Add onion and mushroom. Saute till light golden. Add flour. Cook on low heat for a minute. Do not brown. Add milk gradually, stirring all the time so that no lumps are formed. Add all ingredients given under sauce. Allow it to boil. Taste salt. Remove from fire.

14. Drop tortellini in the white sauce. Toss gently. Serve immediately.

UNUSUAL PASTA RECIPES

Rosemary Chick pea Pasta

*Chick-peas are used and cooked in a variety of ways all over the world.
Here, they are combined with pasta for a great combination.*

Serves 4

1½ cup penne pasta (whole wheat or flour)
3 tbsp butter
½ tbsp crushed garlic
1 tbsp dried rosemary or oregano (preferably rosemary)
5 tbsp grated cheddar cheese

CHICKPEAS AND FETA MIXTURE
½ cup chickpeas (*safed chhole*) - soaked overnight and boiled
4 tomatoes - chopped
1 cup roughly mashed cottage cheese (*paneer*)
2 tbsp balsamic vinegar or 1 tbsp vinegar mixed with a pinch of powdered sugar
½ tsp pepper
½ tsp salt
8 sun–dried tomatoes - chopped (optional)
1 tbsp capers, drained (optional)

1. Boil 8-10 cups of water in a large pan. Add 2 tsp salt and 1 tbsp oil. Drop pasta in boiling water. Boil for 7-8 minutes or till pasta turns soft but is still firm. Remove from fire and let the pasta stay in hot water for 2-3 minutes. Strain. Refresh in cold water and strain again. Leave pasta in strainer for 15 minutes so that all the water drains out. Sprinkle 1-2 tbsp olive oil on the pasta and toss well. Keep aside.

2. Heat butter in a pan, add garlic and pasta. Mix well. Add rosemary.

3. Mix chickpeas, tomatoes, cottage cheese, vinegar, pepper, salt, sun–dried tomatoes and capers in a bowl.

4. Toss chick-pea mixture with warm pasta. Serve sprinkled with cheese (optional).

Stir Fry Black Bean Pasta

Sweet and delicately flavoured, this is the perfect supper for lovers of Chinese food.

Serves 4

2 cups rigatoni or penne pasta

3 tbsp oil

2 spring onions (*hara pyaz*) - chopped till the greens

1 medium green capsicum or 1 red capsicum - cut into juliennes

1 carrot - cut into juliennes

1 tsp salt

½ tsp peppercorns (*sabut kali mirch*) - crushed

1 tbsp chopped & lightly crushed garlic

¼ tsp chilli flakes

½ tbsp soy sauce

5 tbsp black bean sauce (readymade)

¼ cup grated cheddar cheese or cream

1. Boil 8-10 cups of water in a large pan. Add 2 tsp salt and 1 tbsp oil. Drop pasta in boiling water. Boil for 7-8 minutes or till pasta turns soft but is still firm. Remove from fire and let the pasta stay in hot water for 2-3 minutes. Strain. Refresh in cold water and strain again. Leave pasta in strainer for 15 minutes so that all the water drains out. Sprinkle 1-2 tbsp olive oil on the pasta and toss well. Keep aside.

2. Heat 3 tbsp oil in a pan or kadhai. Add white of the onions till it turns light brown. Add garlic. Stir.

3. Add capsicum, carrot, pepper, chilli flakes, salt, soy sauce & black bean sauce. Stir fry on high flame, keeping the vegetables spaced apart, for 3-4 minutes.

4. Reduce heat. Add greens of spring onion, boiled pasta & cheese or cream. Mix well. Serve hot garnished with a little cheese.

Pasta with Sausage in Mushroom Sauce

Beautifully tender sausage slices taste wonderful with a mushroom flavoured pasta sauce.

Serves 4-5

4-5 large chicken sausages - cut into diagonal slices
4 cups bow pasta

MUSHROOM SAUCE
6 tbsp butter, 16 mushrooms (200 gms) - finely chopped
8 tbsp flour (*maida*)
5 cups hot water mixed with 2 stock cubes (seasoning cube)
1 tsp pepper or to taste
2 tsp Worcestershire sauce
6 tbsp ready-made tomato puree
4 tsp tomato ketchup
pepper & salt to taste

1. Boil 8-10 cups of water in a large pan. Add 2 tsp salt and 1 tbsp oil. Drop pasta in boiling water. Boil for 7-8 minutes or till pasta turns soft but is still firm. Remove from fire and let the pasta stay in hot water for 2-3 minutes. Strain. Refresh in cold water and strain again. Leave pasta in strainer for 15 minutes so that all the water drains out. Sprinkle 1-2 tbsp olive oil on the pasta and toss well. Keep aside.

2. To prepare the sauce, heat butter and fry the mushrooms until golden brown. Add sausages and stir fry for a minute.

3. Sprinkle the flour and fry on low heat until brown. Remove from heat. Mix the stock cube in hot water and add to the mushrooms. Add tomato puree and tomato ketchup. Return to fire. Boil. Cook stirring continuously for 8-10 minutes or till thick.

4. Add pasta, mix. Check seasonings and salt. Serve hot.

TiP

Cut sausages diagonally with a crinkle cutter to get beautiful looking slices (see picture). These cutters are easily available in the market. You can use them for cutting vegetables also.

Mustard Cabbage Lentil Pasta

A very different pasta. I never thought lentil and pasta would gel together so wonderfully.

Serves 4

2 cups snake/serpentine pasta - boiled
½ cup split gram lentils (*channe ki dal*)
5 cups shredded cabbage
3 tbsp sweet chilli sauce (ready-made Thai sauce)
1 bay leaf (*tej patta*)
¼ tsp salt, 4 tbsp olive oil
1 tsp mustard seeds (*rai*)
1 tsp crushed garlic
½ tsp red chilli flakes
1 tsp dried thyme
1½ tsp salt, ½ tsp pepper
6 tbsp grated cheese

1. Boil 8-10 cups of water in a large pan. Add 2 tsp salt and 1 tbsp oil. Drop pasta in boiling water. Boil for 7-8 minutes or till pasta turns soft but is still firm. Remove from fire and let the pasta stay in hot water for 2-3 minutes. Strain. Refresh in cold water and strain again. Leave pasta in strainer for 15 minutes so that all the water drains out. Sprinkle 1-2 tbsp olive oil on the pasta and toss well. Keep aside.

2. Wash lentils and place in a saucepan with bay leaf and ¼ tsp salt. Bring to a boil, then reduce heat to low and simmer until lentils are soft but not falling apart (20 to 25 minutes).

3. Heat olive oil in a large pan over medium heat. Add mustard seeds. Let them crackle.

4. Add garlic and chilli flakes and saute for 30 seconds.

5. Add cabbage and toss to combine. Cook over medium-low heat for 5 minutes.

6. Add pasta and sweet chilli sauce. Mix well.

7. Add cooked lentils. Add thyme, salt and pepper.

8. Add grated cheese. Serve hot sprinkled with tomato ketchup.

Peanut Butter Chicken Spirals

Serves 2

200 gm boneless chicken breasts

1½ cups fussili or any other pasta

100 gm snow peas - remove strings

1 tsp sesame oil or olive oil

3 tbsp peanut butter

1 tbsp soy sauce

½ tbsp vinegar

1 tsp grated fresh ginger

½ tsp pepper or to taste

½ tsp salt or to taste

½ tsp tabasco sauce

1. Boil 8-10 cups of water in a large pan. Add 2 tsp salt and 1 tbsp oil. Drop pasta in boiling water. Boil for 7-8 minutes or till pasta turns soft but is still firm. Remove from fire and let the pasta stay in hot water for 2-3 minutes. Reserve ½ cup of pasta water, keep aside. Strain. Refresh in cold water and strain again. Leave pasta in strainer for 15 minutes so that all the water drains out. Sprinkle 1-2 tbsp sesame or olive oil on the pasta and toss well. Keep aside.

2. Put chicken breast with a ¼ tsp salt, 1 tbsp oil and ½ cup water in a microwave oven-proof flat dish. Microwave covered for 4 minutes. Pick out the chicken from the bowl. Reserve the water. Let the chicken cool.

3. Shred chicken, drizzle with ½ tbsp soya sauce.

4. In a pan mix peanut butter, reserved chicken water, ½ tbsp soy sauce, vinegar and grated ginger. Mix well and cook for a minute.

5. Add snow peas, chicken, pasta, pepper, salt and tabasco. Mix well.

6. Add reserved pasta water if required. Check seasonings and remove from fire. Serve hot.

Fusilli with Basil Coriander Pesto

This green pesto sauce is prepared with coriander & walnuts.

Serves 4

2 cups fusilli (125 gm) or any pasta (boiled 4 cups), 1-2 tbsp olive oil
2 flakes of garlic, 3 tbsp chopped walnuts (*akhrot*)
½ tsp salt, ½ cup chopped fresh coriander
½ cup chopped basil, 3 tbsp olive oil or any other cooking oil
3 tbsp finely grated cheese, ¾ cup milk

1. Boil 8-10 cups of water in a large pan. Add 2 tsp salt and 1 tbsp oil. Drop pasta to the boiling water. Boil for 7-8 minutes or till pasta turn soft but is still firm. Remove from fire and let the pasta be in hot water for 2-3 minutes. Strain. Refresh in cold water and strain again. Leave pasta in strainer for 15 minutes so that all the water drains out. Sprinkle 1-2 tbsp olive oil on the pasta and mix well. Keep aside.

2. To prepare the pesto, in a grinder combine garlic, walnuts, salt, coriander, basil, olive oil and cheese. Blend intermittently, stopping after every second so that it does not become a smooth paste. Make a rough paste.

3. In a large saucepan boil water with a tsp of salt, add pasta and cook until soft, yet firm. Drain pasta.

4. To serve, mix milk with pesto sauce in a wok or large pan & boil. Simmer for 1 minute. Add pasta to the pesto, toss well and serve.

Nothing Unusual Yet a Classic Salad

A wonderful light salad that combines all the best flavours.

Serves 2-3

½ cup macaroni or any other pasta

1 orange or sweet lime (*mausami*) - peel segments

¼ cup onion - chopped

¼ cup grated cheddar cheese

2 tbsp sliced black olives

1 bread - toasted in a toaster and cut into 1" square pieces

¼ tsp salt

¼ tsp roasted cumin (*bhuna jeera*) *powder*

a pinch of paprika or pepper powder

1½ tsp balsamic or regular vinegar

1. Boil 8-10 cups of water in a large pan. Add 2 tsp salt and 1 tbsp oil. Drop pasta in boiling water. Boil for 7-8 minutes or till pasta turns soft but is still firm. Remove from fire and let the pasta stay in hot water for 2-3 minutes. Strain. Refresh in cold water and strain again. Leave pasta in strainer for 15 minutes so that all the water drains out. Sprinkle 1-2 tbsp olive oil on the pasta and toss well. Keep aside.

2. Place pasta, onion, cheese, olives, orange, salt, roasted cumin powder, paprika or pepper and vinegar in a bowl and toss to combine. Cover and chill till serving time.

3. To serve, add bread squares. Mix. Serve immediately.

Chicken and Mango Pasta Salad

*Pasta salads are a great addition to a buffet. This one is a substantial one dish meal.
Cooked turkey is a tasty alternative to chicken.*

Serves 4

1 cup boiled bow pasta, ½ cup boiled and shredded chicken
1 cup sliced ripe mangoes
1 spring onion - finely chopped with the greens
2 tbsp chopped fresh coriander
½ tsp freshly ground black pepper
1 tbsp whole grain mustard sauce

MANGO CHUTNEY DRESSING
4 tbsp mayonnaise
4 tbsp sweet mango chutney

1. Boil 8-10 cups of water in a large pan. Add 2 tsp salt and 1 tbsp oil. Drop pasta in boiling water. Boil for 7-8 minutes or till pasta turns soft but is still firm. Remove from fire and let the pasta stay in hot water for 2-3 minutes. Strain. Refresh in cold water and strain again. Leave pasta in strainer for 15 minutes so that all the water drains out. Sprinkle 1-2 tbsp olive oil on the pasta and toss well. Keep aside.

2. Place pasta, chicken and mangoes in a bowl and toss to combine.

3. To make dressing, place mayonnaise and mango chutney in a blender. Blend for few seconds. Remove to a bowl.

4. Put pasta, chicken, mangoes, spring onion, coriander, black pepper and whole grain mustard in a bowl and mix to combine. Spoon dressing over salad and toss well. Cover and chill until required.

Greek Pasta Salad

This light and refreshing salad is the ideal companion for spicy or rich foods.

Serves 4

1 cup soup pasta, see note
3 tbsp olive oil, 1½ tbsp vinegar
1 tsp crushed garlic, 1½ tsp dried oregano
¾ tsp ground black pepper (*kali mirch*)
½ tsp white sugar
pinch of salt or to taste
6-8 cherry tomatoes - halved or 1 big tomato - cut into 1" pieces
1 red or green capsicum - sliced
¼ cup crumbled feta or paneer
½ cup chopped greens of spring onion
6-8 whole black olives

1. Boil 5-6 cups of water in a large pan. Add 2 tsp salt and 1 tbsp oil. Drop pasta in boiling water. Boil for 7-8 minutes or till pasta turns soft but is still firm. Remove from fire and let the pasta stay in hot water for 2-3 minutes. Strain. Refresh in cold water and strain again. Leave pasta in strainer for 15 minutes so that all the water drains out. Sprinkle 1-2 tbsp olive oil on the pasta and toss well. Keep aside.

2. In a large bowl, whisk together olive oil, vinegar, garlic, oregano, black pepper, salt and sugar.

3. Add cooked soup pasta, tomatoes, red capsicum, greens of onions and olives. Toss until evenly coated. Cover and chill for 2 hours or overnight. Check seasonings.

4. Sprinkle feta cheese or cottage cheese and serve.

Note: Soup pasta is very tiny pasta pieces of different shapes.

GLOSSARY OF NAMES/TERMS

Arborio rice	Italian, short grained, sticky rice.
Appetizers	Small tasty bits of food served before meals.
Aubergine	Brinjal/eggplant
Au gratin	Any dish made with white sauce and covered with cheese and then baked or grilled.
Bake	To cook by dry heat usually in an oven or a tandoor.
Batter	Any mixture of flour and liquid, which is beaten or stirred to make a pouring consistency.
Beat	To mix with a fast rotatory motion so that air is incorporated into the mixture. Beating makes the mixture light and fluffy.
Blanch	To remove skin by dipping into hot water for a couple of minutes. e.g. to blanch tomatoes or almonds.
Blend	To combine two or more ingredients.
Brinjal	Aubergine/eggplant/baingan
Capsicums	Bell peppers
Caramelize	To heat sugar till it turns brown.
Consistency	A term describing the texture, usually the thickness of a mixture.
Coriander	Cilantro
Cornstarch	Cornflour
Cream	In sauces, half and half will do, in desserts use whipping or heavy cream.
Cut and fold	To mix flour, cream or egg whites very gently into a mixture using a downward and upward movement.
To dust	To sprinkle flour in an empty greased tin so that the cake does not stick to the tin during baking.
Dot	To put small amounts of butter.
Dice	To cut into small neat cubes.
Dough	A mixture of flour, liquid etc., kneaded together into a stiff paste or roll.
Drain	To remove liquid from food.
Garnish	To decorate.
Marinate	To soak food in a mixture for some time so that the flavour of the mixture penetrates into the food.
Plain flour	All purpose flour, maida
Puree	A smooth mixture obtained by rubbing cooked vegetables or blanched tomatoes through a sieve.
Saute	To toss and make light brown in shallow fat.
Sift	To pass dry ingredients through a fine sieve.
Toss	To lightly mix ingredients without mashing them e.g. salads.
Whip	To incorporate air by beating and thus increase the volume as in egg whites and whipped cream.

INTERNATIONAL CONVERSION GUIDE

These are not exact equivalents; they've been rounded-off to make measuring easier.

WEIGHTS & MEASURES

METRIC	IMPERIAL
15 g	½ oz
30 g	1 oz
60 g	2 oz
90 g	3 oz
125 g	4 oz (¼ lb)
155 g	5 oz
185 g	6 oz
220 g	7 oz
250 g	8 oz (½ lb)
280 g	9 oz
315 g	10 oz
345 g	11 oz
375 g	12 oz (¾ lb)
410 g	13 oz
440 g	14 oz
470 g	15 oz
500 g	16 oz (1 lb)
750 g	24 oz (1½ lb)
1 kg	30 oz (2 lb)

LIQUID MEASURES

METRIC	IMPERIAL
30 ml	1 fluid oz
60 ml	2 fluid oz
100 ml	3 fluid oz
125 ml	4 fluid oz
150 ml	5 fluid oz (¼ pint/1 gill)
190 ml	6 fluid oz
250 ml	8 fluid oz
300 ml	10 fluid oz (½ pint)
500 ml	16 fluid oz
600 ml	20 fluid oz (1 pint)
1000 ml	1¾ pints

CUPS & SPOON MEASURES

METRIC	IMPERIAL
1 ml	¼ tsp
2 ml	½ tsp
5 ml	1 tsp
15 ml	1 tbsp
60 ml	¼ cup
125 ml	½ cup
250 ml	1 cup

HELPFUL MEASURES

METRIC	IMPERIAL
3 mm	1/8 in
6 mm	¼ in
1 cm	½ in
2 cm	¾ in
2.5 cm	1 in
5 cm	2 in
6 cm	2½ in
8 cm	3 in
10 cm	4 in
13 cm	5 in
15 cm	6 in
18 cm	7 in
20 cm	8 in
23 cm	9 in
25 cm	10 in
28 cm	11 in
30 cm	12 in (1ft)

HOW TO MEASURE

When using the graduated metric measuring cups, it is important to shake the dry ingredients loosely into the required cup. Do not tap the cup on the table, or pack the ingredients into the cup unless otherwise directed. Level top of cup with a knife. When using graduated metric measuring spoons, level top of spoon with a knife. When measuring liquids in the jug, place jug on a flat surface, check for accuracy at eye level.

OVEN TEMPERATURE

These oven temperatures are only a guide. Always check the manufacturer's manual.

	°C (Celsius)	°F (Fahrenheit)	Gas Mark
Very low	120	250	1
Low	150	300	2
Moderately low	160	325	3
Moderate	180	350	4
Moderately high	190	375	5
High	200	400	6
Very high	230	450	7

India's No.1 Cook Books

FREE HOME DELIVERY

011 2325 0091
011 2325 2948

(within India)

NITA MEHTA COOKERY CLUB

Become a **MEMBER**

Get **FREE** Cookbooks

buy online at:

www.nitamehta.com

www.nitamehta.com